# THE
# MAGIC LIBRARY
# Great
# Card Tricks

Bruce Smith

Sterling Publishing Co., Inc.
New York

Editor: Shona Grimbley
Consultant Magicians: Anthony Owen and Marc Paul
Designer: Graham Curd at wda
Illustrator: Colin Woodman

**Library of Congress Cataloging in Publication Data Available**

10 9 8 7 6 5 4 3 2 1

Published by Sterling Publishing Company, Inc.
387 Park Avenue South New York, NY 10016
First Published in Great Britain
under the title *Card Tricks*
© 1995 Arcturus Publishing Limited/ Bruce Smith
Distributed in Canada by Sterling Publishing
c/o Canada Manda Group, One Atlantic Ave, Suite 105,
Toronto, Ontario, Canada M6K 3

ISBN 0-8069-7175-4

# Contents

Glossary of Terms                4
Self-Working Card Tricks         6
Fake Cards                      30
The Glide                       54
Big Effects                     72

Advanced Card Tricks            79
Can't Go Wrong                  81
Forces                          94
Controlling Cards              101
The Stacked Pack               117
Card Classics                  130
Basic Card Controls            145
Index                          159

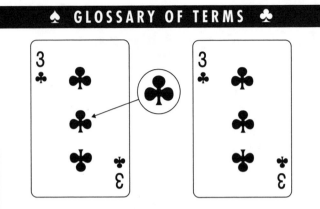

PIPS

SPOT CARD

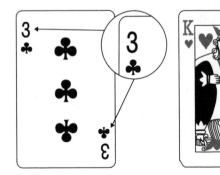

INDICES

COURT CARD
or PICTURE CARD

DEALING
POSITION

FAN OF
CARDS

CUTTING
THE PACK

COMPLETING
THE CUT

# SELF-WORKING
# CARD TRICKS

**Effect** *A spectator chooses any card from three poker hands by just thinking of it. The magician correctly identifies the chosen card.*

**Preparation** *No preparation is needed for this effect.*

● ● ● ● ● ● ● ● ● ● ● ● ● ● ● ●

**1** Have the cards shuffled by the spectator while you explain that when gambling a poker player must always have an expressionless face – hence the term "poker face." Deal three hands of seven cards each, face up.

**2** As you deal out the three hands, explain that you can find a spectator's chosen card by studying their facial expressions. Concentrate on the hands for a moment. Then ask a spectator to JUST THINK of any one card in any of the hands. Ask which hand the chosen card is in.

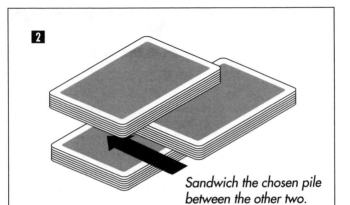

*Sandwich the chosen pile between the other two.*

**3** Collect up the three hands and sandwich the pile containing the chosen card between the other two.

**4** Deal out the same 21 cards into three face-up hands of seven cards, and again ask which pile contains the chosen card. Collect up the cards as before, sandwiching the indicated hand between the others. Explain to your audience once more how you should be able to tell which is the chosen card by looking at the spectator's face. Just a flicker of an eyelid or a twitch of an ear can

### TOP TIPS FOR TRICKSTERS

*Never repeat a trick for the same audience. The surprise is lost the second time and they will watch you more closely!*

give them away.

**5** Repeat this dealing, questioning and sandwiching once more. The selected card will now automatically be the 11th card from the top.

**6** Deal the cards one at a time on to the table face up, looking at the spectator. When you get to the 11th card, hesitate. Then dramatically show the audience the

*The chosen card is the 11th from the top.*

**3**

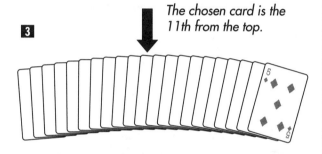

### THE HOOKER RISING CARDS

*Many magicians used to believe that this effect, like the Indian Rope Trick, was a myth. The story was that in 1918 an amateur magician, Dr Hooker, put on a show during which he made selected cards rise out of a pack and float up in the air. Although the secret of this effect was lost for nearly 80 years, in November 1993 a Californian magician and illusion builder performed the Hooker Rising Cards at the 3rd Los Angeles Conference of Magic History.*

**Effect** *A card flies invisibly from one pile to another.*

*This trick works automatically. Try it out on a friend, following the instructions carefully.*

• • • • • • • • • • • • • • • •

**1** Ask your friend to hold out their hands as in illustration 1 with their knuckles touching the table.

**1**

**2** From your pack of cards put two cards into each gap between the fingers, except for the last gap, into which you put only ONE card – THE ODD CARD.

**3** Starting from the left, remove each pair of cards and split them. Place them separately on the table making two piles (illustration 3).

**4** Repeat this with all the pairs – splitting them and adding one card to each pile. Point out that two is an even number.

**2** *Put two cards in each gap, except for the last gap.*

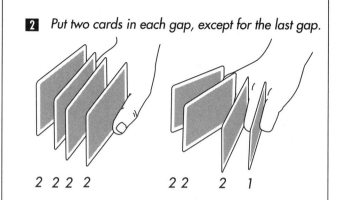

*2 2 2 2*          *2 2*     *2*     *1*

**5** Ask your friend to choose one pile. Explain that you will add the odd card to the pile they choose. When they have selected a pile, bury the odd card somewhere in the middle. Point out that this pile is now odd and the other is even.

**6** Replace the cards from the "odd" pile in pairs between the fingers of one hand, as you did originally – amazingly all the cards will be paired up and the odd card has vanished.

### TOP TIPS FOR TRICKSTERS

*Always practice what you are going to say with your tricks. This is known as the magician's "patter" and should be rehearsed just as carefully as the working and method of the trick.*

**3** *Deal the cards into two equal piles.*

**7** Point out that there were an even number of cards. Your friend has two hands, ten fingers, eight gaps between them – all even numbers. The only odd thing in the trick is the one card which seems to have vanished.

**8** Replace the "even" pile in pairs between the fingers of the other hand. You will be left with one odd card. It appears as though it has magically jumped across.

### HARRY HOUDINI (1874-1926)

*Although he later became famous for his daring death-defying escapes, in his early days in show business Houdini was billed as the "King of Kards" (sic). He would perform sleight-of-hand card tricks similar to the ones described in this book. Even when he was a world famous "escapologist" he would still feature card tricks in his stage performances.*

## ♥ THE INVISIBLE DICE ♦

**Effect** *The magician spreads six cards out across the table and a spectator is given a sealed prediction. The magician gives a second spectator an invisible dice and asks them to roll it across the table top and call out the number it shows! Whatever the number they call the magician's prediction is correct!*

**Requirements** *You need five blue-backed cards – the Ace, Three, Four and Six of Clubs and the Five of Hearts. You will also need one red-backed card – the Two of Clubs. In addition, write a prediction which reads "You will choose the red card."*

**Preparation** *Put the cards into a pile which runs from top to bottom as follows – the face-down Three of Clubs, the face-up Ace of Clubs, the face-down Five of Hearts, the face-up Four of Clubs, the face-down Six of Clubs and the face-up Two of Clubs.*

• • • • • • • • • • • • • • • •

**1** Deal out the cards from the pile from left to right. Explain to the audience that you have six cards – one to

**1**

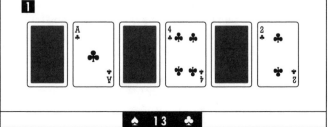

**2** *The cards turned the other way up.*

six – three face up and three face down. Tell them they will see why in just a moment (illustration 1).

**2** Ask a member of your audience to act as safekeeper for your prediction envelope.

**3** Reach into your pocket and mime removing your invisible dice. Tell your audience that this is the world famous invisible dice. "It is the only one in the world. Well, if there is another one, I've never seen it!"

**4** Hand it to a member of the audience. Choose someone who you think will go along with the act and join in. It's no fun if they just stare at you and say "There's nothing there," so choose carefully.

**5** Ask them to roll the dice across the table top. Tell them not to throw it too hard, or it might fall on the floor and take ages to find! When they have rolled the dice ask them what number they have on top. "Are you happy with that number or do you want to roll it again to make sure it's not loaded?" When they have decided on a number ask someone to read out the prediction, and continue for your big finish as in step 6.

**6** i) If they choose number one, point to the Two of Clubs at the far right of the row. Tell them this is number one. Turn all the cards face down to show that it is the only red backed card!

ii) If they choose number two, point to the Two of Clubs. Again, turn all the cards face down to show that the two is red backed!

iii) If three is chosen count from left to right and show the third card is the Five of Hearts. Turn all the other cards face up to show it is the only red one out of the six!

iv) As for three, but count from right to left!

v) If five is chosen turn all the cards face up to show the Five of Hearts is the only red one!

vi) If six is chosen count from left to right and show the "sixth" card is the only one with a red back!

YOU WILL CHOOSE THE RED CARD

**TOP TIPS FOR TRICKSTERS**

*When you perform try to relax and stand naturally. Don't fidget or shuffle your feet.*

**Effect** *A pile of cards are mixed to a spectator's instructions, but end up in their original order.*

**Requirements** *For this you will require all 13 cards from one suit.*

**Preparation** *Set the cards in order Ace through to King as in illustration 1.*

● ● ● ● ● ● ● ● ● ● ● ● ● ● ● ● ●

**1** Spread the cards out face up on the table, as in illustration 1, to display the cards in suit order. Now explain to the audience that any casino will tell you that most of the traditional ways that cards are handled aren't particularly secure! Cutting cards does not change the order of the cards and there are many false shuffles to enable you to control the order of the cards while

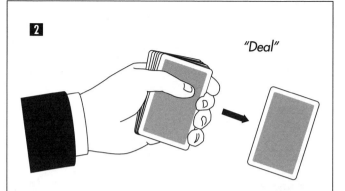

"Deal"

shuffling them. However, there is a method of really mixing cards which you will demonstrate that is called the *Duck and Deal*.

**2** Gather up the pile face down in the dealing position and ask the spectator if they want you to deal or duck the first card. If they say "Deal", simply deal the card face down on the table (illustration 2). If they say "Duck", slide the first card under the second card (illustration 3) and place them both face down on the table (illustration 4).

### TOP TIPS FOR TRICKSTERS

*Always practice in front of a mirror or a video camera so that you can see exactly how your tricks will look to your audience.*

*"Duck"*

*Second card*

*First card*

*The second card goes on top of the first – then both cards go on the table.*

**3** Ask the spectator if they want to deal or duck the new top card of the pile, and continue – following their instructions at every step – right through the pile. As far as the audience is concerned it now seems as if the cards have been mixed in a haphazard way, and you should emphasise that at each step it is the spectator's choice whether they wish to duck or deal. If you try this yourself you will be convinced that you have thoroughly shuffled

---

**TOP TIPS FOR TRICKSTERS**

*Try to use a pack of cards which have a "linen" finish (this is usually marked on the box), as these are the easiest cards to handle.*

the cards, but if you go through the pile you will be surprised to discover that in fact the cards are now in reverse order.

**4** Collect up the cards from the table, keeping them face down, and repeat the process, going through the pile asking "Duck" or "Deal" with each card. Repeating the action adds to the effect and gives the impression that the cards are thoroughly shuffled. In fact what this

*Both top cards go on the table.*

second process does is to return the cards to the order they were in at the start of the trick.

**5** At the end, after following all the spectator's instructions as to whether they want each card ducked or dealt on to the table, you should recap by saying, "The choice throughout has been yours. You have been the magician – I have only been the spectator following your instructions. You would expect the cards to be really mixed up, but as you are the magician please now say a few magic words . . ." (You may find it necessary to suggest a few magic words to them, if they seem at a loss.)

**6** After the spectator has said the magic words, deal out the cards face up, one at a time. Deal slowly at first, then get faster and faster. This will increase the drama as the cards are shown to be in the same suit order as they began!

### CARDINI (1899-1973)

*Cardini was the stage name of the Welsh born magician Richard Pitchford. He found fame after he moved to America where he toured the theatres performing an act of flawless card manipulations, apparently plucking fans of cards from thin air. At the height of his fame he returned to London (where he had once been the manager of the magic department in the famous shop Gamages) to star in a Royal Variety Command Performance.*

**Effect** *A card is chosen from a pile and the magician successfully identifies it.*

**Requirements** *For this effect you can only use the cards shown in illustration 2. You are able to tell whether these cards have been turned around because the majority of the pips point one way – either up or down. This explains why they are called One Way Cards.*

**Preparation** *Arrange the cards beforehand so the majority of the pips on the cards all point the same way.*

● ● ● ● ● ● ● ● ● ● ● ● ● ● ● ●

**1**

*All these suits point up.*

**1** Start by having the cards thoroughly shuffled. Show the audience that the cards are all different and then fan them face down for one to be freely selected.

**2** When a card is selected and looked at, watch carefully to ensure that it is not accidentally turned upside down. When you have performed this effect a few times you will notice that the spectator nearly always returns the card the same way round that it was taken.

**3** Before the card is replaced turn the pile around in your hand so that the pips on the cards will now be pointing the other way. Do not look at your hands as you do this. To distract the audience, say casually that the spectator could have chosen any one of the cards, and fan the cards again so the audience can see they are all different. Do not look at the cards, or the audience will accuse you of cheating! Ask the audience to remember the card chosen, and make sure everyone has seen it. This is a good time to turn the pile around as the audience is now more interested in the chosen card than in what you are doing. This is a basic form of magician's misdirection.

**4** Ask the spectator to replace the selected card anywhere in the pile. It is now simple for you to find this card by dealing the cards face up and looking for the one with the pips pointing in a different direction (see illustration 3).

**3**

*Most pips point
<u>towards</u> performer.*

*Most pips point
<u>towards</u> performer.*

*On the selected card
most pips point
<u>away</u> from performer.*

**Effect** *A spectator has a free choice of four piles of cards. The magician has accurately predicted which pile would be selected.*

**Requirements** *Write a prediction, as in illustration 2, reading "YOU WILL CHOOSE THE SEVEN PILE." You also need four face-down piles of cards containing i) the four Sevens; ii) any seven odd value cards; iii) two Threes and an Ace; and iv) an Eight, Six, Four and Two.*

• • • • • • • • • • • • • • • •

**1**

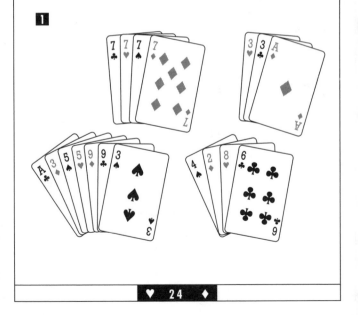

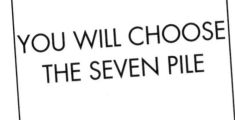

YOU WILL CHOOSE
THE SEVEN PILE

**1** Ask a spectator to select any one of the four-face down piles. Assure them they can change their mind until they finally settle on one chosen pile.

**2** If they choose i), ii), or iii) ask them to read the prediction. You now have an "out" for each pile. If they chose i) show they picked the only pile with the four sevens. If they chose ii) count the cards face down to show it is the only pile containing seven cards. And if they chose iii) show that it is the only pile in which the values add up to seven.

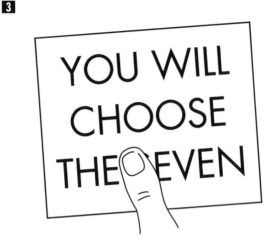

**3** If they chose iv) you pick up the prediction and display it – as in illustration 3 – keeping your thumb over the "S" so that it appears to read: "YOU WILL CHOOSE THE EVEN PILE." Show that their selected pile is the only one which contains even cards. Whichever pile they choose it seems as though you knew all along!

### TOP TIPS FOR TRICKSTERS

*Your tricks will always have more impact if you "routine" three or four of them together to make a short show.*

## ♥ CLOCK TOWER CARD ♦

**Effect** *A spectator freely selects the only red card in the pack – and proves your prediction correct.*

**Requirements** *Remove all the black cards and one single red card from the pack (the value of the red card does not matter). Discard the rest of the pack.*

**Preparation** *Prepare a prediction (as in illustration 3) which reads "YOU WILL <u>NOT</u> CHOOSE A BLACK CARD." Put the red card in the 13th position from the top of the pile.*

• • • • • • • • • • • • • • •

**1**

*The prepared pile has 26 black cards and 1 red.*

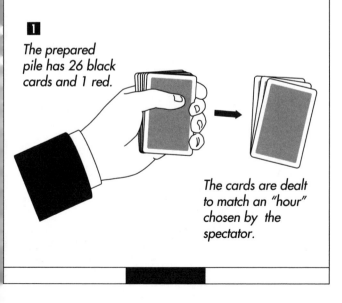

*The cards are dealt to match an "hour" chosen by the spectator.*

**1** Put the prediction face down on the table. In this effect do not let the audience see the face of the cards.

**2** Ask someone to picture a clock tower and imagine it chiming any hour. Ask them to take the pile of cards where you can't see them and count off the number of cards that matches their chosen hour (i.e. between one and twelve). They keep the cards they have dealt off and hand you back the rest of the pile.

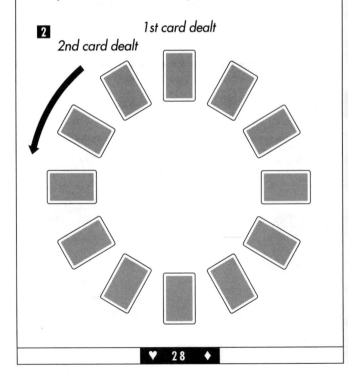

*1st card dealt*

*2nd card dealt*

**3** Deal cards off the top of the pile around the table to make a clockface (illustration 2). Start at the 12 o'clock position and deal the next 11 cards round anti-clockwise to make the face.

**4** Ask the spectator what time they chose, and turn over the card in that position. It will be the red card. Ask them to read out the prediction. The chances are they will not be impressed as this is just a 50/50 chance.

**3**

YOU WILL <u>NOT</u>
CHOOSE
A BLACK CARD

**5** But when you reveal that all the other cards in the clockface, in their hand and in the pile are black cards, then they will be impressed!

# FAKE CARDS

**All the tricks in this section are accomplished using fake cards which can be easily made at home.**

**Effect** *The four Queens are shown singly. They each magically transform into the corresponding Four. Everything can then be examined.*

**Requirements** *You will need to make a fake card by carefully cutting out the two shaded areas marked in illustration 1 from a Queen of Hearts. In addition to this fake card you will need the four Fours.*

**Preparation** *Arrange the five cards in a pile face up with the Four of Hearts on top and the fake Queen on top of that, giving the illusion that this is a complete Queen of Hearts. The cut-out areas in the Queen will not be noticed by the spectator. The heart in the Four of Hearts is in the right position to complete this deception.*

● ● ● ● ● ● ● ● ● ● ● ● ● ● ●

**1** Hold the pile squared in the left hand and display to the audience the face card, apparently a regular Queen of Hearts.

**2** Turn the left hand over so that the backs of the cards are uppermost, and with your right hand reach under the pile. Apparently you are going to slide out

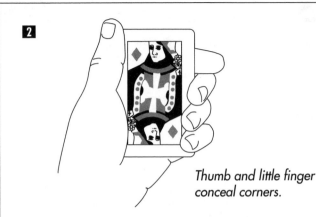

*Thumb and little finger conceal corners.*

the Queen of Hearts face down. In reality your right fingers contact the Four of Hearts through the hole in the Queen and push the Four out of the pile. Grab the card with the right hand and, keeping it face down, place it on the table.

**3** Turn the pile in the left hand back face up. You now appear to show a Queen of a different suit. Illustration 2 shows how your left thumb and fingers can cover the unmatching corner indices.

**4** Repeat the process of reversing your left hand and pulling out the next Four, and placing it face down on the table. Do the same with the next Four. As you place each card on the table dramatically name it. Do not rush this. Make sure the audience can see your hands are empty and not holding any extra cards.

**5** After displaying the final suit place the card, with the back outwards, in your pocket. Leave the genuine card sticking out as in illustration 3, and let the fake card secretly slip down inside your pocket.

**6** Ask your audience to keep an eye on the Queen in your pocket and an eye on the three Queens on the table. Ask them if they can remember the suit of the Queen in your pocket or any of the Queens on the table. They may manage to get the names of the suits correct – but tell them they should have been watching the values more closely. Show them the card in your pocket has turned into a Four. Then ask a spectator to turn over the three cards on the table. To the amazement of the audience these have turned into Fours as well.

*Fake card slips down into pocket. Last Four pulled out and shown.*

**Effect** *A message appears magically on the face of the Joker under impossible conditions.*

**Requirements** *For this you require two identical Jokers, a few extra cards and an elastic band.*

**Preparation** *Prepare one of the Jokers by writing a suitable message on it as in illustration 1. Add this Joker to the face of the pile and put the elastic band around the whole pile.*

*Cut the other Joker in half and discard the bottom half. The elastic band holds the half Joker in position covering the secret message, so the card appears to the audience as a single complete joker.*

• • • • • • • • • • • • • • • •

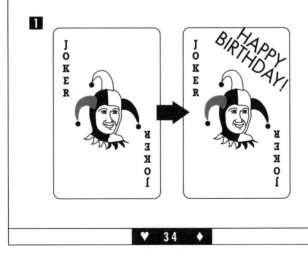

**2**

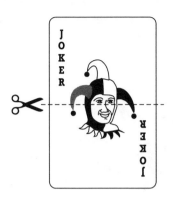

*Cut the second Joker in half.*

**1** Show the Joker on the face of the pile. Tell the audience that the Joker is very clever. In fact, the Joker is actually the most intelligent card in the pack. He has a degree in spelling . . .

**2** Turn the pile over and pull the genuine Joker out from under the elastic band (illustration 4). Ensure that you keep the Joker face down. Ask a spectator to keep their hand on top of the Joker. Take the same pen or pencil you used to write on the card and place it under their hand next to the Joker.

### TOP TIPS FOR TRICKSTERS
*Never turn your back on an audience – that's when they might sneak out!*

**3** Discard the rest of the pile. Take care that the audience do not see the half Joker on the face of the pile as you place it to one side.

*An elastic band holds the half Joker in place.*

**4** Now turn the Joker face up to show that a message has magically appeared! . . . proving that this really is the world's most intelligent Joker.

**5** You can make any suitable message appear on the card. For example, you could have "Happy Birthday", "Congratulations", or the name of your client or your company!

**6** An even more impressive effect is obtained by combining this effect with the Clock Tower trick, so that you can apparently make the name of a freely chosen card appear on the face of the Joker. You can have fun by pretending that the Joker is also a magician. Explain that he is going to do the trick by reading the minds of your friends.

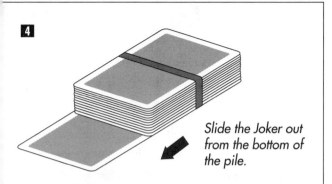

*Slide the Joker out from the bottom of the pile.*

### DAI VERNON (1894-1993)

*Dai Vernon is still affectionately remembered by magicians as "The Professor" because of his apparently endless fountain of magical knowledge. Born in Canada, by the age of 12 Vernon had mastered all the sleight-of-hand tricks in the classic book on card handling – The Expert at the Card Table. Vernon fell in love with magic and spent the rest of his life baffling everyone with his ability. At top nightspots in New York he performed his elegant Harlequin Act, which concluded with him filling the stage with live butterflies! He turned down the opportunity to become a famous stage magician and became a lecturer and author on his true love – close-up sleight-of-hand and card magic. He spent the last 30 years of his life in Hollywood, as a mentor for many great close-up magicians. He died aged 98.*

**Effect** *This is a variation of the famous Three Card Trick or Monte, often known as Find the Lady. The spectator fails to find the Queen as it vanishes from the fan.*

**Requirements** *You will need one Queen and three ordinary (not court) cards. Cut off one edge of the Queen and sellotape it on to one of the ordinary cards to make a flap (illustration 1). This is your fake card.*

**Preparation** *Set the cards up in a fan, with the fake card with the Queen flap at the bottom. Insert one of the ordinary cards under the flap (as in illustration 2) and the other card goes on top to cover everything. It should appear that the Queen is in the center of the fan (see illustration 3).*

• • • • • • • • • • • • • • •

**1**

*Stick Queen flap to the other card with a hinge of sellotape between the Xs.*

**1** Display the fan face up to your audience. Point out the Queen in the center. Explain that the Three Card Trick or Find the Lady has been used to win money for many years. You can see it performed all over the world, in Times Square in New York, at racecourses, in bars – anywhere that card sharpers and conmen think

**TOP TIPS FOR TRICKSTERS**

*Never force your tricks on your friends.*
*Wait until they ask to see them.*

that they can win some money.

**2** Turn the fan face down and ask a spectator to remove the card they think is the Queen. They will remove the center card. If you are careful not to reveal the flap you

**3**

can show the other two ordinary cards.

**3** When the spectator turns over the card they believe to

---

**TOP TIPS FOR TRICKSTERS**

*Have a look through the tricks in this book to see if you can put together your own act.*

---

be the Queen, they will discover it has changed. They have been caught once again! If you wish, you can write a surprise personal message on the card. You could write, "You owe me $100" or "I hope that's

**4**

*Spectator removes the middle card.*

### JOHANN N. HOFZINSER (1806-1875)

*The Austrian Hofzinser was one of the first to transform card magic from the tricks of low conmen into sophisticated artistry. He frequently performed his sleight-of-hand magic for gentry and royalty. He created and developed many original effects, routines and plots which are still performed by close-up magicians around the world today. His book* Hofzinser's Card Conjuring *is a classic among lovers of card magic.*

## ♠ CALCULATOR CARD ♣

**Effect** *The magician calculates that a freely chosen card is six and three-quarters from the top – and it is!*

**Requirements** *Tear off a quarter of a card, to give you three-quarters of a card (see illustration 1).*

**Preparation** *Set the "three-quarters" card face down on the table and deal six more cards face down on top of it. Add one face-up card on top to be your indicator card (the Two of Clubs in illustration 1). This seven and three-quarter card set-up goes beneath the rest of your face-down pack.*

● ● ● ● ● ● ● ● ● ● ● ● ● ● ● ● ●

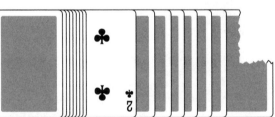

**1** Fan the cards out face down for a spectator to select one. As you do this, be careful you do not fan too far and expose the face-up card.

**2** Ask the spectator to remember the card and place it face down on top of the pack.

**3** Ask the spectator to cut the pack wherever they like. Ask them to complete the cut (illustrations 2 and 3). Apparently the card is lost somewhere in the center of the deck. In reality your prepared stack is on top of it.

**2**

Ask your audience if they think it would be a good trick if you went through the pack and found one card face up – and that was the freely selected card. They will probably agree that it would.

**4** Say to them that you do not do good tricks – you only do miracles! Fan through the pack face down to reveal your face-up card. Cut it to the top. When the spectator says it is not their selection, explain that it is your calculator card that will calculate where their selection is. Pretend to listen to the face-up card and then announce the total is "six and three-quarters"! When you say "six and three-quarters" look slightly embarrassed, and look at your calculator card as though it really did talk to you. Apologise to your audience and say that the calculator card must be having an "off day." Once again you ask the calculator card the position of the chosen card. Again you pretend that it says "six and three-quarters." This a very funny situation with you talking and disagreeing with the calculator card.

**5** Deal six cards off the top of the pack and then display the three-quarters card. The next card will be the chosen card. The calculator card is always correct!

**3**

**Effect** *A fan of four Kings changes into the four Aces!*

**Requirements** *For this effect you will need four Aces, four Kings, a Joker, some scissors and some glue. To make the special fake cards cut the four Kings diagonally in half from the bottom left to the top right corner (illustration 1). Glue half of each King into position on the corresponding Ace (illustration 2). Now the cards can be fanned to show either the four Kings or, when fanned the other way, the four Aces.*

**Preparation** *Set up the cards with all the Kings in the top left hand corner and the Joker on top (illustration 3).*

● ● ● ● ● ● ● ● ● ● ● ● ● ● ● ●

**1**

**1** Display the Joker and explain that in many games the Joker is wild and can be used to represent any card. It is almost as if the Joker changes into any card. Explain that you can use your magical powers to do this to any card! Say that if you were playing a game of poker, a hand with four Kings and a wild Joker would be very good and you would probably bet a large amount of money on the outcome of the game.

### TOP TIPS FOR TRICKSTERS

*Never get talked into showing tricks that you haven't rehearsed fully.*

**2** Fan the cards to show the four Kings – as in illustration 3. The Joker covers the split on the face card.

**3** Square the cards up and turn them around in your hand. Say your magical incantation and explain that

although you know the only hand that can beat your hand is the four Aces, you are going to use your magical powers to make sure you cannot be beaten. When you fan out the cards (illustration 4) they have changed into the four Aces. Wow!

You can use this same half card principle to apparently print blank cards (stick blank card on to the face of four cards as you did with the Kings). You can tell the tale of the Joker being a magical printer who changes

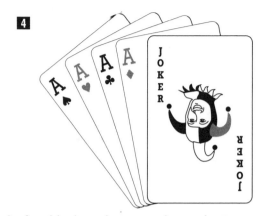

the four blank cards into regular cards. Or you could say how you made sure that you won a game of cards by making all the other player's cards vanish.

### JEAN HUGARD (1872-1959)

*Hugard was an Australian magician who performed all over the world, before finally making his home in America. In his stage show he featured the famous Bullet Catch effect. This is a highly dangerous and dramatic effect which has claimed the lives of 12 magicians. However, it is probably as an author that he is best remembered today, particularly for his highly recommended works with Fred Braue on card magic – The Royal Road to Card Magic and Expert Card Technique.*

*They seek him here, they seek him there,*
*those Frenchies seek him everywhere.*
*Is he in heaven? Or is he in hell?*
*That darned elusive Pimpernel.*

**Effect** *The "scarlet" court card vanishes from a pile of three cards.*

**Requirements** *For this effect you will need three spot cards and one court card.*

**Preparation** *Cut the court card in half widthways and stick it on to the back of one of the spot cards (illustration 1). Discard the other half of the court card.*

● ● ● ● ● ● ● ● ● ● ● ● ● ● ● ●

**1** Step the three cards in your left hand, as in illustration 2, so that the half court card is showing in the middle. Explain that the court card represents the famous Scarlet Pimpernel.

**2** Pull out the card behind the court card (the Two of Diamonds in illustration 2). Turn it face down and slide it back behind the court card (illustration 3), but slide it square with the center card. Now turn the pile over.

**3** Pull out the face down card which is sticking out (illustration 4). In our effect this is the Two of Hearts. Turn it

**2**

**3**

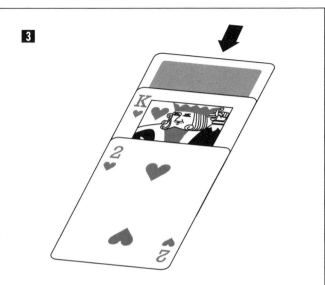

face up and replace it face up behind the other two cards (illustration 5). Turn the pile face down again.

**4** Holding the cards in your left hand step the three cards away from you to show three backs as in illustration 6. Ask a spectator to guess which one of the cards is the court card. Most people will select the middle card but it doesn't matter if they don't.

**TOP TIPS FOR TRICKSTERS**

*It is always good to finish with your best trick.*

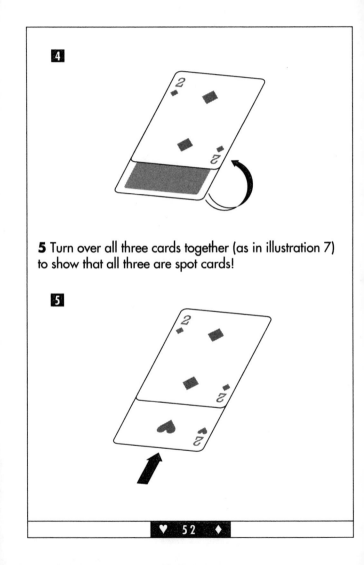

**4**

**5** Turn over all three cards together (as in illustration 7) to show that all three are spot cards!

**5**

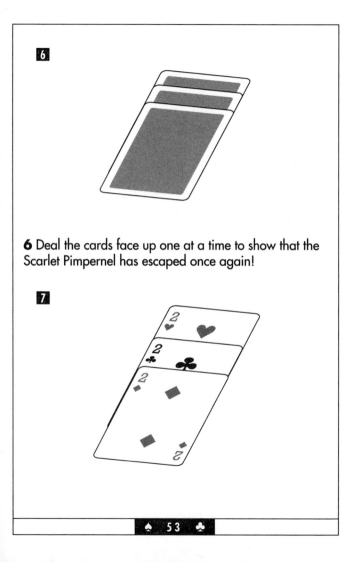

**6** Deal the cards face up one at a time to show that the Scarlet Pimpernel has escaped once again!

# THE GLIDE

*The glide move enables you to secretly substitute one card for another. First we will teach you the move, and then some tricks which use it.*

● ● ● ● ● ● ● ● ● ● ● ● ● ● ●

**1** Hold a pile of cards in your left hand in the position shown in illustration 1. This displays the face card to the audience. Notice that your little finger of the left hand is curled around the edge almost touching the face card (the Two of Diamonds in the illustration).

**1**

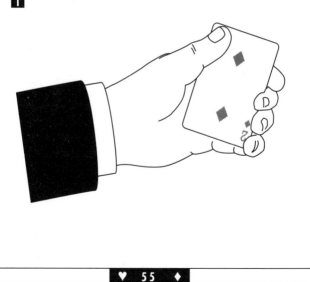

**2** Turn your left hand over so that the cards are face
down (as in illustration 2). You are apparently going to
pull out the face card, that the audience has just seen,
from the bottom. In fact you will actually pull out the
card second from bottom. This is similar to the move you
used for the Queens to Fours trick – but without a hole in
the card!

**3** Your left little finger contacts the face card and pulls it
backwards a little way. Illustration 3 shows this secret
movement from underneath.

**4** Now it is simple for your right hand to reach under
the pile and slide out the card which is one from the
bottom (illustration 4). The audience believes this to be

**3**

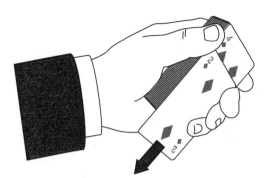

the card which they saw on the face a moment before. If you have difficulty pulling back the card with just the little finger you can use the right fingertips to push it back when they reach under to pull out the card.

As you will see in this section there are many great tricks you can do with this move, so it is worth learning and practicing it until you can do it perfectly.

### TOP TIPS FOR TRICKSTERS

*Your audience will be more impressed if you do just one or two tricks really well, than several tricks poorly.*

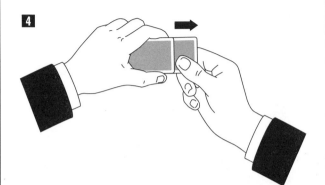

4

**Effect** *This effect shows you how you can use the glide move to force a card.*

**Requirements** *You can use any pile of cards.*

**Preparation** *Set the cards so that you know the name of the bottom card.*

• • • • • • • • • • • • • • • •

**1** Hold the cards face down in your left hand in position for the glide move. Do not let the audience see the card on the face.

**1**

**2** Ask a spectator to call "stop" at any time while you deal cards on to the table. Tell them that the card they call stop on is the one you will use.

**3** Perform the glide move with your little finger (illustration 1). With your right hand pull the second card from bottom of the pack and deal it face down on to the table (illustration 2).

**4** Reminding the spectator that they can call "stop" any time they wish, continue dealing keeping the known card – the force card – pulled back. Each time it is the card second from the bottom you deal on to the table.

### TOP TIPS FOR TRICKSTERS
*Use a new pack of cards for each performance.*
*Grubby old cards look unprofessional.*

**5** When they say "stop", your right hand takes the real bottom card – your force card – and pulls that forward from the bottom of the pile (illustration 3). Hand this to the spectator. Even though they called stop whenever they wanted you can reveal the name of their card.

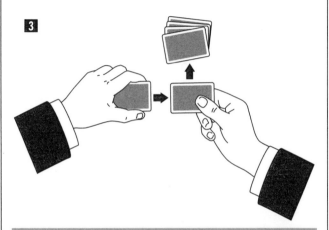

### RICKY JAY

*This outrageous Californian performer must be the only person to become the talk of New York and the theater's "hot ticket" with a show consisting primarily of card tricks! His one-man show "Ricky Jay and his Fifty-Two Assistants" was an Off-Broadway hit in 1994. Jay also holds the World Record for throwing single playing cards the greatest distance.*

**Effect** *A spectator attempts – unsuccessfully – to follow the magician's simple instructions.*

**Requirements** *For this you require eight cards – four for you and four for your assistant.*

• • • • • • • • • • • • • • • •

**1** Hold your cards in your lefthand face-down glide position. Get a friend to copy all your actions with their pile of cards. Ask them, "How good are you at following instructions? I have a simple test for you using just four cards. And if you do well you could win a prize!" At this point offer them a suitable outlandish prize like a new car or a round-the-world cruise.

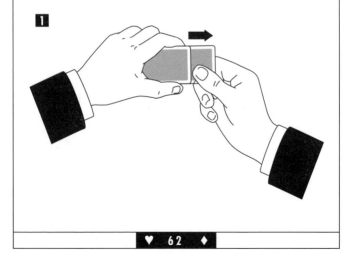

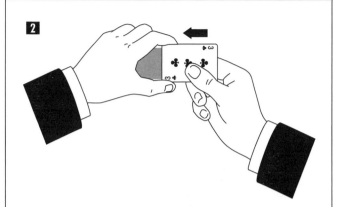

**2** Say, "Now watch very carefully. All I do is . . . " Slide out the bottom card, turn it face up and place it on top of the pile (illustrations 1 and 2). Get your friend to do the same.

**3** Slide out the new bottom card and place it on top without reversing it. Your friend does the same.

**4** Slide out the new bottom card, turn it face up and place it on top of the pile. Your friend does the same.

**TOP TIPS FOR TRICKSTERS**

*Remember that when you are performing card tricks your audience will be watching your hands closely. Make sure they are clean!*

*Performer's cards
when dealt on the table.*

Turn both piles over.
**5** Slide out the bottom card and deal it on to the table to show it is face down. Perform the glide move and show your next card is also face down. Fan the top two cards to show they are both face up. Because your friend does not know about the secret glide move their cards will be

---

**TOP TIPS FOR TRICKSTERS**

*Make sure you have a clean dry surface to work on. It might be worth buying a small piece of carpet to use as your "close-up mat".*

---

**TOP TIPS FOR TRICKSTERS**

*Never tell your audience what you are about to do.
It spoils the surprise and they will know if things don't
go according to plan!*

**4**

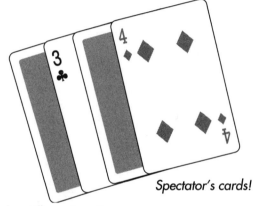

*Spectator's cards!*

mixed up (illustration 4).
Even though they followed you exactly they still got it
wrong!

**6** You can repeat this with someone else or do it with a
group of people – each with four cards – all trying, unsuccessfully, to follow you. If you do repeat this over and over
again it is a good idea to get progressively faster and
faster. The more people that are involved, the better it will
look. And as it gets faster it will seem more and more
comical to the audience watching and those participating.

**Effect** *The spectator fails an observation test as a card magically changes.*

**Requirements** *For this you will require the four Kings and one odd card. We have chosen to use an Ace in the description. It is the Ace of Hearts in the illustration.*

**Preparation** *Set the pile face down with the Ace on top of the four Kings. The spectators must not know how many cards you have.*

● ● ● ● ● ● ● ● ● ● ● ● ● ● ● ●

**1** Hold the pile in the left hand in the face-down glide position. Pull out the first King from the bottom of the pile and place it face up on the table. Pull out the second King and drop that face up on top of the first King.

**2** Perform the glide on the next card (illustration 1) and, with the right hand, pull out the top two cards squared together as one (illustration 2). This is made easy by the glide. It appears you are just showing another King. Drop the two cards, as one, face up on to the pile on the table (illustration 3).

**3** Finally display the last King and drop it face up on top of the pile. Pick up the pile apparently containing just the four Kings and mix the cards, keeping the faces towards you. You need to end up with the Ace in the third position and the King of the same suit on the top of the face-down pile. Challenge the audience to remember the order of the cards. Normally this would be quite simple – but when you shuffle them it becomes almost impossible to know the order.

**4** Hold the pile, as you began, in the lefthand face-down glide position. Repeat the actions you did earlier – first card on table, second card on table, glide, double card on table – until you are left with one face-down card in your hand. Ask the audience to guess the suit of each card before you deal it on to the table. If they guess correctly, congratulate them. If they get it wrong, tell them to try harder. Finally you will get to the point where you have just one card left in your hand. Surely they can guess which card it is now, as they can see the other "three" cards face up on the table. The audience believe this to be a King. In fact it is the Ace.

**5** Explain that this is an observation test. Which card do they think you are left with? After they have guessed show them that the final King has changed into an Ace. Let them examine the Ace while you scoop up the cards from the table.

**3**

**Effect** *The four Aces are inserted into different parts of the pack, but to prove the magician's claim that they are "inseparable Aces" they all move next to each other in the pack.*

**Requirements** *A normal pack of 52 cards.*

**Preparation** *None.*

●●●●●●●●●●●●●●●●

This is another effect using a full pack which makes use of the glide move you have already learnt.

*All the Aces are put behind cards of the same value.*

**1**

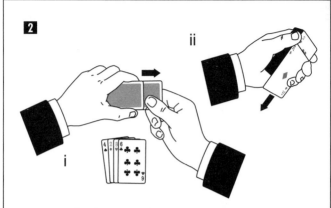

**1** Remove the four Aces from the pack and place them face up on the table.

**2** Evenly fan the pack in your left hand keeping the faces of the cards towards you.

**3** Insert the four Aces into the pack. You apparently do this at random, but in reality all four Aces go to the left of cards of the same value. For example, all the Aces are inserted into the pack next to a Seven (as in illustration 1). These cards will be known as your indicator cards. The cards must be on the right of the Ace. Push the Aces square into the fan and square up the fan. The four Aces are apparently lost in the pack, but you know the cards which come before them.

**4** Explain that the four Aces are inseparable and now you are going to prove it. Hold the pack face down in the left hand in glide position. Pull out the bottom card with the right hand and place it face up on the table. Do the same with the next card and continue through the pack (illustration 2 i) until you reach the first of your indicator cards that you know are next to the Aces. When you have dealt this card on to the table perform the glide move on the bottom card (illustration 2 ii). You know this bottom card will be one of the Aces because it was next to one of your indicator cards.

**5** Keeping the first Ace pushed back, continue pulling out the cards above it one at a time and dealing them face up on to the table as you did before, until you reach the next of your indicator cards. When you have dealt the indicator card push the next card back with

your right fingertips. This will put the first two Aces together. Then continue pulling out the cards above them. . .

**6** Do the same thing after the third indicator card – pushing back the Ace with your right fingertips. When you pull out the final indicator card you know it is time to pull off all four Aces from the bottom of the pack – one at a time. All four Aces have moved together in the pack, proving they really are "inseparable Aces"!

# BIG EFFECTS

**These are card tricks which could be used on a platform
or stage and still be effective.**

**Effect** *The magician makes three cards fly invisibly from the pack to join ten cards inside a sealed envelope, which a spectator is sitting on!*

**Requirements** *For this you will need at least 20 cards and an envelope.*

**Preparation** *Secretly prepare for this effect by placing three cards inside the envelope (illustration 1).*

• • • • • • • • • • • • • • • •

**1** Ask someone to deal ten cards from the pack. Drop these cards into the envelope and ask someone to sit on them. Unknown to the audience there are now 13 cards in the envelope.

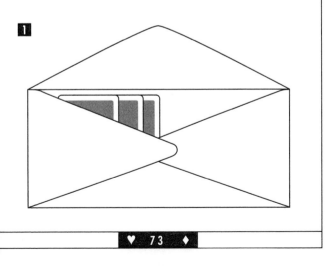

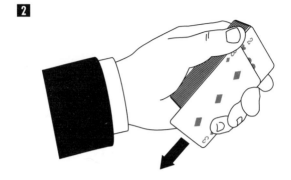

**2** You announce that you need a number to be randomly selected by a member of the audience. The number chosen will indicate the number of cards to fly magically into the envelope. Using the glide force you can make someone stop you on a three-spot card (illustration 2). Alternatively you can just announce that you are going to make three cards pass invisibly from the pack into the envelope which the spectator is sitting on.

**3** Mime throwing three cards from the pile towards the person sitting on the envelope. You can have a lot of fun by getting the audience to participate by pretending to pass the cards along. You could ask the person sitting on the envelope if they felt the cards arrive. For example, you could pretend that the first card is palmed in the right hand. Hold the right hand with the back to the audience as though it was secretly concealing a card. You say, "Of course if you do that you must not tell anyone or let them catch a glimpse of the card in your hand." As you say this you turn your right hand to show it really is empty. Explain the card is invisible and mime throwing it towards the envelope.

**4** Apparently tie the second invisible card on to a length of invisible string, and ask your assistant sitting on the envelope to reel in the string and place the card in the envelope. Silly as it may seem, they usually enjoy doing this and hamming it up will earn you a few more laughs from the audience.

**5** Explain that the third card is the toughest of them all. Take another invisible card from the pack and throw it into the air. Pretend to follow its invisible flight around the room – "and it lands in that gentleman's pocket!" Indicate a man in the audience, but as he reaches into his pocket continue quickly, "but it doesn't stop there!" The card crawls down his leg, along the floor and up into the envelope.

**6** Ask your assistant to open the envelope and count aloud the number of cards now inside the envelope. Amazingly there are now 13. Do not ignore this trick because of its simplicity – it will have people talking for a long time after your performance.

**TOP TIPS FOR TRICKSTERS**
*Always make sure that your flies are done up!*

**Effect** *A spectator manages to select the only card from a contrasting suit. It looks as if the magician has goofed – but it all ends up okay.*

**Requirements** *For this you need 26 cards – two complete color contrasting suits. In the description we use Hearts and Clubs. You will also need a prediction (illustration 3) and some Copydex glue.*

**Preparation** *To prepare for this you will need to lightly glue a red card on to the back of each black card so that you have 13 double cards. You only need a couple of dabs of Copydex on the back of each black card to do this (illustration 1). You also need a written prediction saying "YOU WILL CHOOSE A HEART".*

**1**

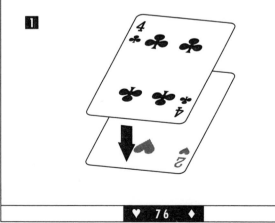

**1** Hand the sealed prediction to someone to guard it for you. Tell them that no-one is to go near the prediction. If you are doing this trick on a stage it is better to invite the volunteer on to the stage to look after the envelope so that everyone can see all is fair and above board. They are to read it out when you ask them.

**2** Ask someone on stage to assist you. Explain that you have predicted which suit they will choose. As you say this fan the cards to the audience. They will only see clubs in the fan (illustration 2). This will get a laugh when they realise how you are going to trick your assistant!

**3** Do not show the faces of the cards to your assistant on stage, but ask them to touch the back of any card. Make sure they keep their finger on it as you cut it to the top of the pile.

**4** Peel the top card off of the back of the Club. Because you have only used a couple of spots of glue it should separate quite easily. Hand them this card, but don't let anyone see the face of it.

**5** Ask your prediction keeper to read out what it says. When they do you should get another big laugh from the audience, who only saw Clubs. Pretend that the trick has gone wrong. Ask the spectator who was looking after the envelope if anyone has changed the envelope for another one. Ask them if they are trying to ruin your trick? The prediction should say that they would choose a black card, a Club.

**6** Everything ends with a big laugh when your assistant on stage turns the card around to reveal they chose the only Heart (apparently!) from all those Clubs. This will get another big laugh and hopefully a well deserved round of applause. All's well that ends well!

**3**

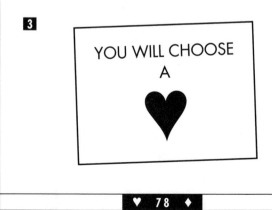

# ADVANCED
# CARD TRICKS

# CAN'T GO WRONG!

**The tricks in this section are all self-working, easy to do and require no sleight of hand. You need only a full pack of cards.**

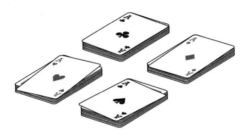

**Effect** *The spectator cuts the pack into four piles – and the top card of each pile is an Ace!*

**Requirements** *You require a full pack of 52 cards.*

**Preparation** *To prepare, secretly set the four Aces face down on top of the pack.*

• • • • • • • • • • • • • • • •

**1** Ask a spectator if they feel lucky. Ask them to cut the face-down pack into four roughly equal piles – A, B, C and D. It is important to keep an eye on the pile that contains the four Aces (pile D).

**1**

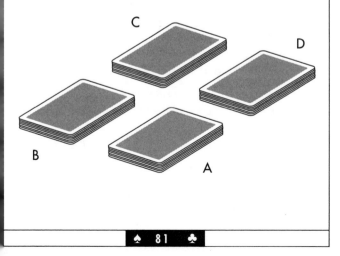

**2** Ask the spectator to pick up the first pile (pile A) and move the top three cards from the top of the pile to the bottom (illustration 2). Then ask them to deal a card from the top of pile A on to each of the other three piles (B, C and D). This is shown in illustration 3. Explain that this procedure is to make sure the cards are really thoroughly mixed and the cuts are truly random.

**3** Have pile A placed back on the table and repeat the above process with each of the remaining three piles in

---

### TOP TIPS FOR TRICKSTERS

*If a trick goes wrong – don't worry, just move on to your next trick. The audience will only be bothered about it if they think you are!*

**3**

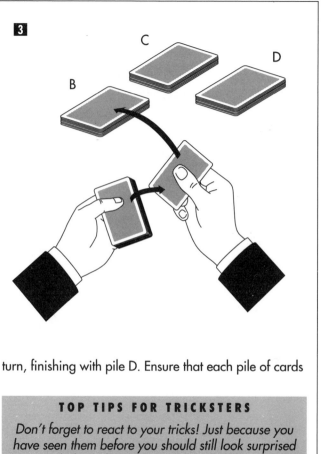

turn, finishing with pile D. Ensure that each pile of cards

**4**

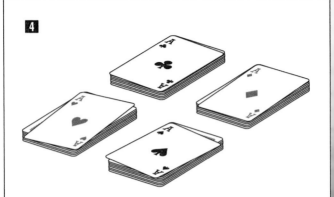

is replaced in its original position.

**4** When this has been completed with all four piles ask the spectator to turn over the top card of each pile. They will be amazed to find the four Aces (illustration 4). It must be their lucky day! Suggest that they book their

## NATE LEIPSIG (1873-1939)

*Nate Leipsig was a rarity – a vaudeville top-of-the-bill act who had an incredible sleight-of-hand technique. Originally an optician, he became a professional magician and gained a reputation as much for his close-up magic as for his stage performances. He frequently gave stunning performances for royalty and high society, and was very much considered to be the "magician's magician."*

**Effect** *The spectator is able to correctly name a card the magician chooses!*

**Requirements** *All you need is a full pack of 52 cards.*

**Preparation** *This requires no secret preparation.*

• • • • • • • • • • • • • • • •

**1** Explain that the spectator is going to do this trick themselves! Ask them to shuffle and mix the cards as much as they like. You now need to select a card. Ask them to fan the cards face towards you. Tell them that you are going to remove a card you have been dreaming about. In actual fact the card you remove is decided by the top two cards of the pack.

**1**

**2** Look at the fan and note the value of the first card and the suit of the second (illustration 1). Now look for the card that matches that combination of suit and value. For example, if the top card is the Four of Clubs and the second card the Queen of Hearts you will look for the Four of Hearts. Remove this card and put it face down to one side. Tell the spectator they now have to discover the name of the card. They will have no idea how to do this, so you offer to help. Explain that they have to work out the suit and the value of the card.

**3** Ask them to hold the pack face down and deal the cards one at a time face down on to the table to make a single pile (illustration 2). They can stop dealing whenever they wish – the choice is theirs. When they have finished dealing ask them to discard the rest of the pack. They will only need the cards in the pile on the table. These are the cards which will enable them to identify the name of your "dream card."

**3**

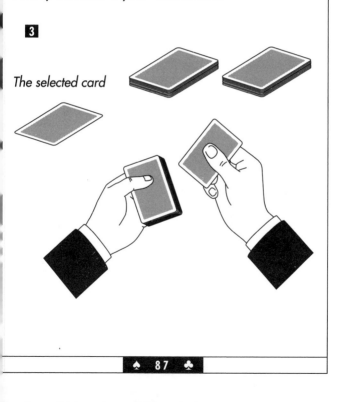

*The selected card*

**4** Explain that your card, like all cards, is made up of two things – a suit and a value. Ask them to pick up the pile of cards and deal them face down into two piles – a suit pile and value pile (illustration 3). They must deal alternately as they would in a game of cards until all the cards from their pile have been used up.

**5** Ask them to turn over the top card of each pile (illustration 4). These will be the two cards which began on top of the pack and told you which card to select! One will indicate the suit, the other the value. The spectator can now tell you the name of the card you chose. Turn over your selected card to show they are correct and lead the applause for them! Ask them if there are any other dreams of yours they can tell you about!

**4**

**Effect** *Two face-up cards are inserted into the face-down pack. Incredibly they prove to be next to their matching partner!*

**Requirements** *All you need is a full pack of 52 cards.*

**Preparation** *There is no special preparation needed for this effect.*

• • • • • • • • • • • • • • • •

**1** Fan the pack and note which cards are at the top and bottom (illustration 1). Then openly remove the two cards that are their twins (that is, are of the same colour and value – as are the Six of Hearts and the Six of Diamonds). Put these two cards face up on the table.

**2** Hand the face-down pack to a spectator and ask them to deal cards one at a time face down on the table (illustration 2). They can stop whenever they wish – the choice is theirs. When they stop, drop the first matching card (the one that matched the bottom card) face up on top of the card they stopped on. Ask them to drop the rest of the pack face down on top (illustration 3).

### TOP TIPS FOR TRICKSTERS

*You can misdirect people by using their names. When you mention someone's name they will look up at your face and away from your hands.*

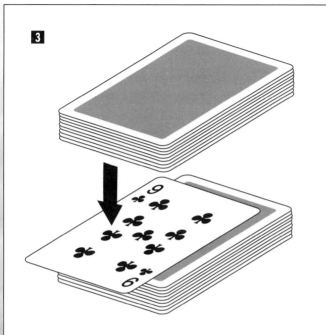

**3** Ask them to pick up all the cards and deal again, one at a time, face down as before. They can stop whenever they wish. When they stop, drop the second "twin" card

face up where they stopped and get them to drop the rest of the pack face down on top. Explain that twins often match up in mysterious ways, even if they are separated and the odds are against them. One twin may feel pain when the other is hurt, or they may know each other's thoughts. They frequently end up meeting when they least expect it.

### TOP TIPS FOR TRICKSTERS

*Wash your hands before you rehearse or perform. It helps to keep your props clean and last longer, and makes you look good too!*

## 5

**4** Spread the pack face down across the table (illustration 4). Despite the fact that the spectator could have stopped dealing whenever they wished, the next face-down card above each of the face-up cards will be their Gemini twins (illustration 5)! Spooky stuff – the twins match up once again!

### HISTORY OF PLAYING CARDS

*The first printed playing cards were produced from engravings around 1500. The cards were round and featured the suits of flowers, wild men, birds and deer – and there was a fifth suit of lions and bears.*

# FORCES

This section will teach you how you can "force" a card on a spectator who apparently has a free choice.

**Effect** *After correctly naming a chosen card the magician finds a straight, a royal flush and three Aces!*

**Requirements** *A regular pack.*

**Preparation** *Set the following cards face down on top of the pack: Four of Spades, Five of Spades, Six of Spades, Seven of Spades, Eight of Spades, Nine of Spades, Ace of Hearts, Ace of Clubs, Ace of Diamonds, Ace of Spades, King of Spades, Queen of Spades, Jack of Spades, Ten of Spades (illustration 1).*

**1**       *The Four of Spades is on top of the pack.*

**1** Ask a spectator to name any number between ten and 20 (TEN TO TWENTY FORCE). Deal their selected number of cards into a face-down pile (A) alongside the pack (illustration 2).

**2** Add together the two digits of their selected number to make a new total. For example if they chose 16 add one and six to make seven. Deal off the new number of cards from pile A to make a third face down pile (B). Show your spectator the last card dealt. Although apparently a random selection, this is always the Ace of Spades. This is because of the Ten to Twenty force.

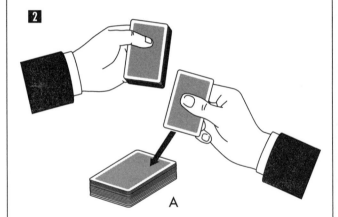

A

### TOP TIPS FOR TRICKSTERS

*If you are having problems rehearsing a trick don't worry about it. Leave it for a while and come back to it later on when you are fresh.*

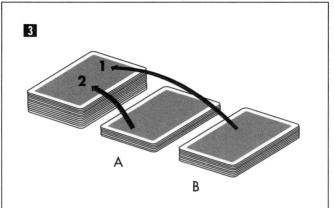

**3** Place the Ace of Spades face down on top of pile B and drop pile B cards on top of the pack. Then drop pile A on top of the pack (illustration 3).

**4** Having revealed that the chosen card was the Ace of Spades, offer to deal to it by magic. Deal off the top three cards into a pile. Then deal the next six cards into a second pile. The next card will be their chosen card – the Ace of Spades.

**5** You offer to go "just a little bit further" and show how you do this. You turn over the pile of three cards on the table – these are the three Aces. You then turn over the pile of six cards to reveal they are the Four, Five, Six, Seven, Eight and Nine of Spades!

This is a self-working trick that always has a big impact and is a good way to learn the classic TEN TO TWENTY

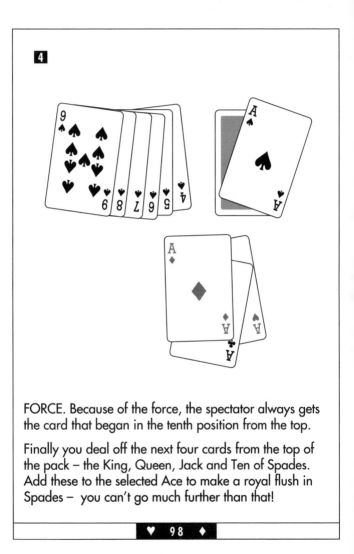

FORCE. Because of the force, the spectator always gets the card that began in the tenth position from the top.

Finally you deal off the next four cards from the top of the pack – the King, Queen, Jack and Ten of Spades. Add these to the selected Ace to make a royal flush in Spades – you can't go much further than that!

**Effect** *A selected card magically appears stuck on the outside of a window!*

**Requirements** *A full pack of 52 cards, plus an identical duplicate of the card to be "forced".*

**Preparation** *Before the performance, secretly stick your duplicate card on the outside of a nearby window. For best results use double-sided sticky tape. It is best to stick the card near the corner of the window so that it is slightly covered by the curtain or blinds inside – this will reduce the possibility of anybody noticing the card before your performance. You will be surprised, as I frequently am when I you perform this effect, how people do not notice the card stuck on the window. Ensure the force card is on top of the pack.*

● ● ● ● ● ● ● ● ● ● ● ● ● ● ●

**1**

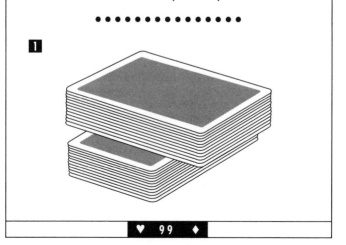

**1** Hold the pack face down in your open hand. You are going to perform the classic cross-cut force. Ask a spectator to cut the pack anywhere they like and set their cut cards face down on the table. Drop the cards in your hand on top at right angles to the rest of the pack, creating the cross-cut (illustration 1).

**2** Now you talk about the freedom of their selection. In reality the card they cut to is now on top of the pack, but they soon forget this. Lift off the cards you just set on top and hand them the top card of the bottom half. This is actually your force card that began of top on the pack! This is an amazingly deceptive force and requires absolutely no sleight of hand!

**3** Now the hard work is done! You ask them to shuffle their card into the pack so that you cannot know its position.

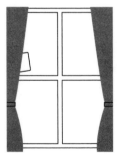

**4** When they are happy, throw the pack of cards at the window which has the card stuck on the other side (illustration 2). Watch their amazement as they try to remove their card and discover it is stuck on the outside! This is one of the most powerful tricks in the world of magic – and you will have a lot of fun with it.

# CONTROLLING CARDS

Instead of forcing a card you can use "key" cards to discover the
position of a freely selected card.

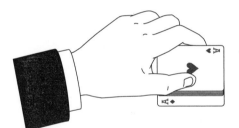

**Effect** *The magician knows when a spectator is lying and correctly names the card they selected.*

**Requirements** *You will need a full pack of 52 cards.*

**Preparation** *There is no preparation for this trick.*

• • • • • • • • • • • • • • • •

**1** Ask a spectator to freely select a card from the face-down pack.

**2** While they are looking at their card, you secretly look at the bottom card of the pack (illustration 1). This is

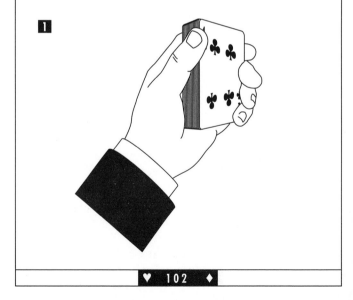

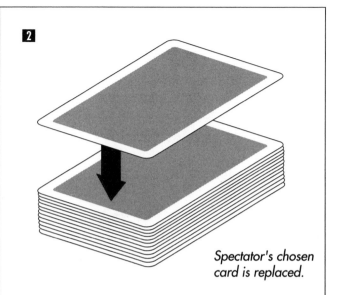

## 2

*Spectator's chosen card is replaced.*

known as "glimpsing" a card, as you secretly catch a glimpse of it. Remember the identity of the glimpsed card. We will assume it is the Four of Clubs.

**3** Ask the spectator to replace their card face down on top of the pack (illustration 2). Explain that you are going to use a lie detector to discover the name of their selected card! You do not need any special equipment, just your magical powers. At the moment though it is easy as you know their card is on top of the pack! The card needs to be hidden somewhere in the middle.

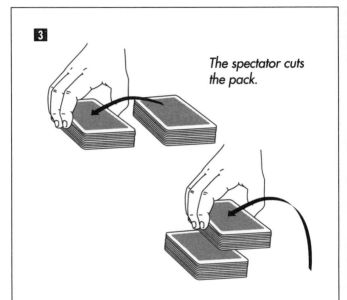

**3**

*The spectator cuts the pack.*

**4** Get the spectator to cut the pack wherever they like and to complete the cut by placing the bottom half on top. Unknown to them this puts their selected card next to your known "key" card (illustration 3).

**5** The pack can be cut and the cut completed as many times as the spectator wishes as this will not mix the order of the cards – but the pack must not be shuffled!

**6** Spread the cards face up across the table and pretend to read the spectator's mind. Tell them to lie when you reach their card (illustration 4).

**7** Point to a few different cards, asking, "Is this your card?" Point to the card above your "key" card. This will be their selected card. Ask them again, "Is this your card?" When they lie and say, "No", tell them they are

**4**

*chosen card*

### ALEX ELMSLEY

*A quiet, unassuming gentleman, Elmsley is the inventor and creator of some of the best card magic of the twentieth century. Never a professional magician (he was a computer analyst by profession), he concentrated on creating new effects, methods and sleights which continue to have a resounding impact on the world of magic. Following his recent retirement he has become a regular visitor to the Magic Circle.*

**Effect** *The magician correctly identifies a selected card – first fooling his audience into thinking he has made a mistake.*

**Requirements** *You need only a full pack of 52 cards.*

**Preparation** *There is no preparation for this trick.*

• • • • • • • • • • • • • • •

**1** Ask a spectator to freely select a card from a face-down fan of cards.

**2** While your audience are looking at the card secretly glimpse and remember the bottom card of the pack (illustration 1).

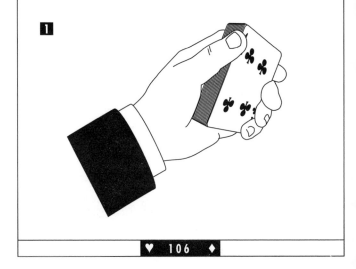

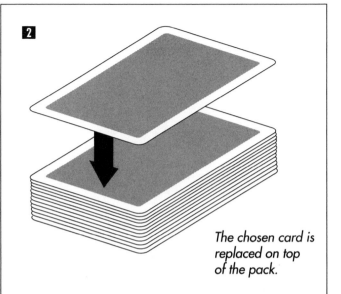

*The chosen card is
replaced on top
of the pack.*

**3** Ask the spectator to replace the card face down on
top of the pack (illustration 2). Explain that in a moment
you are going to deal through the cards, turning them
over one at a time, and you will know instantly exactly
which card they selected. If nothing else, the audience
should be impressed with your confidence! This bold
claim helps to set them up for when the trick appears to
go wrong. In fact, you point out, you are so sure you
can do it, you might even be willing to bet on it!

**4** Ask the spectator to cut the pack and complete the cut.
This places your key card next to their selected card.

**5** Holding the pack face down in your left hand deal the cards one at a time face up on to the table (illustration 3). The card dealt after your key card will be the selected card, but continue dealing a few more cards on top of this. The audience will assume you have missed the card and got the trick wrong.

### TOP TIPS FOR TRICKSTERS

*Don't embarrass your volunteers or make them look foolish – they could mess up the trick and make you look even worse!*

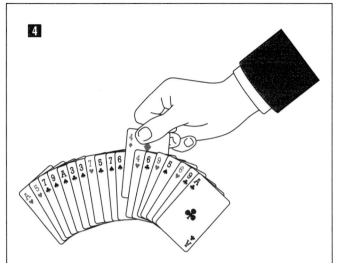

**6** Stop dealing and say that you are willing to bet that the next card you turn over will be their card. As they have seen you pass their card they will be enthusiastic to bet. Once you have agreed the stakes reach into the pile of face-up cards, pull out their selected card and turn it face down (illustration 4). If you are the conscientious type you can return their stakes and say that you'll settle for a packet of crisps. If you want to make enemies, then grab the money – and run!

---

**TOP TIPS FOR TRICKSTERS**

*Always make sure that your fingernails are clean!*

---

*In the next two tricks we use another type of key card called the thick short card. This is made by sticking two cards together (face to back) and trimming a tiny sliver off one end. The Jokers are ideal for this. When this thick card is in the pack you can flick through it and hear a distinct "clunk" when you reach the thick card.*

**Effect** *Using your super sensitive fingers you find the selected card while the pack is in your pocket.*

**Requirements** *A full pack of 52 cards and one thick card.*

**Preparation** *Begin with the thick card on the bottom of the pack.*

• • • • • • • • • • • • • • • •

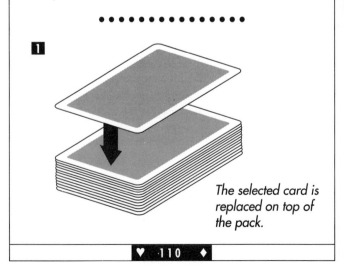

*The selected card is replaced on top of the pack.*

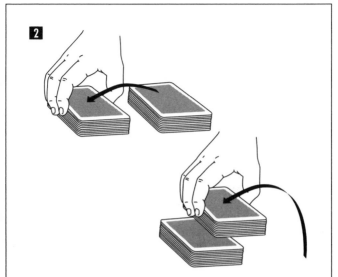

**1** Fan the cards face down. Ask a spectator to select a card, remember it, and replace it face down on top of the pack (illustration 1).

**2** Ask the spectator to cut the pack and complete the cut (illustration 2).

**3** Flick down the pack until you hear the "clunk" and cut at that point. This secretly brings the thick card to the bottom and the selection to the top.

**4** Explain that you are going to drop the pack into your pocket and, using only your sensitive fingertips, find the spectator's selected card. This sounds impressive, but it is actually very easy as you know the card is on top of the pack!

**5** Place the pack in your pocket and then thrust your hand inside. Pretend to have difficulty finding the card and then pull out the top card (illustration 3). Show that it is the selected card.

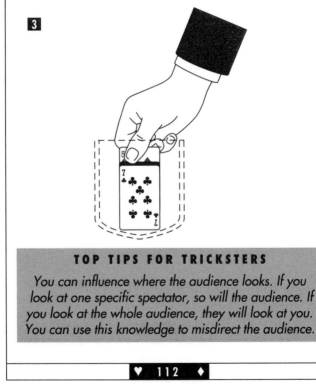

### TOP TIPS FOR TRICKSTERS

*You can influence where the audience looks. If you look at one specific spectator, so will the audience. If you look at the whole audience, they will look at you. You can use this knowledge to misdirect the audience.*

**Effect** *A selected card appears sandwiched between two face-up Aces.*

**Requirements** *A full pack of 52 cards and one thick card.*

**Preparation** *Begin with the thick card on top of the pack. Remove the two red Aces and place them on the table to one side.*

● ● ● ● ● ● ● ● ● ● ● ● ● ● ● ●

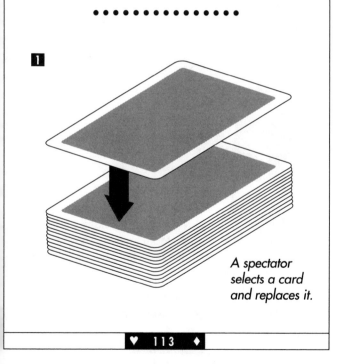

*A spectator selects a card and replaces it.*

**1** Fan the cards face down.

**2** Ask a spectator to choose a card, remember it and replace it face down on top of the pack (illustration 1).

**3** Ask the spectator to cut the pack and replace the bottom half on top, completing the cut. Take back the pack. Flick down the pack until you hear the "clunk" and cut at that point. This brings the thick card to the top and the selected card to the bottom of the pack.

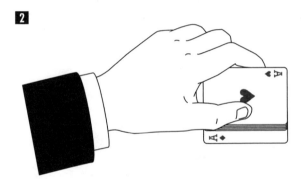

**4** Hold the pack face down in your left hand and place the first red Ace face up on top. Place the second red Ace on the bottom, so that it is sticking out slightly to the left (illustration 2).

**5** Hold the top card with your left thumb and the bottom card with your left fingers. Secretly your left fingertips

also contact the face of the selected card (illustration 3). Explain to your audience that you need absolute silence for this trick as it is very difficult and has taken many years of constant sleight-of-hand practice (and it would do too if you didn't have the thick card!). Build up the tension as you tell them that the two Aces are going to sandwich their selected card in mid-air. It all sounds very impressive!

### TOP TIPS FOR TRICKSTERS

*Make a checklist of where all your props are at the start of your act. Refer to it each time you set up for a show to make sure everything is where it should be.*

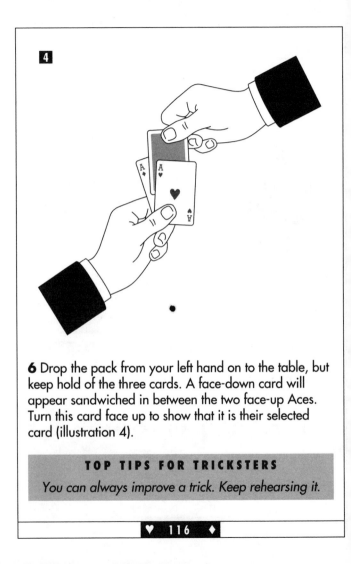

**4**

**6** Drop the pack from your left hand on to the table, but keep hold of the three cards. A face-down card will appear sandwiched in between the two face-up Aces. Turn this card face up to show that it is their selected card (illustration 4).

# THE STACKED PACK

**A "stacked" pack is a full pack set in a prearranged order,
enabling the magician to know the position of any card.**

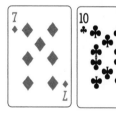 

**Requirements** *A full pack of 52 cards set up in the order shown in illustration 1.*

• • • • • • • • • • • • • • • •

**1** The simplest stack to learn is the one known as the "Si Stebbins" system. The order of the cards is given in illustration 1.

**2** By studying illustration1 you will see how it is always possible to work out what the next card in the sequence will be. Simply add three to the value. Count Jacks as 11, Queens as 12 and Kings as 13. The suits appear in the order of Clubs, Hearts, Spades, Diamonds. You can remember this by thinking of the word CHaSeD, which features the initial letters in order.

**3** Set up your pack in the "Si Stebbins" order and familiarize yourself with the system. You can always work out what the card on the top of the pack will be by glimpsing the bottom card. You will be amazed how fast you can get the knack of the system.

**4** You are now ready to move on to the other effects in this section.

### TOP TIPS FOR TRICKSTERS

*Always be sure to give clear instructions to your volunteers to avoid confusion.*

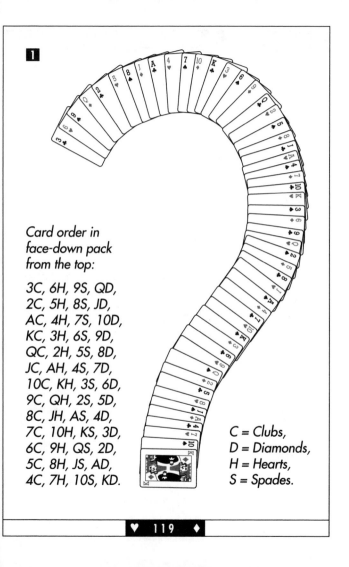

**1**

*Card order in
face-down pack
from the top:*

*3C, 6H, 9S, QD,
2C, 5H, 8S, JD,
AC, 4H, 7S, 10D,
KC, 3H, 6S, 9D,
QC, 2H, 5S, 8D,
JC, AH, 4S, 7D,
10C, KH, 3S, 6D,
9C, QH, 2S, 5D,
8C, JH, AS, 4D,
7C, 10H, KS, 3D,
6C, 9H, QS, 2D,
5C, 8H, JS, AD,
4C, 7H, 10S, KD.*

*C = Clubs,
D = Diamonds,
H = Hearts,
S = Spades.*

## ♠ STACKED SELECTION ♣

**Effect** *The magician correctly names a selected card before it is even returned to the pack!*

**Requirements** *You need a full pack of 52 cards.*

**Preparation** *Set up the pack in "Si Stebbins" order.*

• • • • • • • • • • • • • • • •

**1** Show that the cards are all different and fan them face down for a card to be selected.

**1**

*Cut cards go to the bottom of the pack.*

**2** Cut the pack where the card is taken. Cut the cards above the selection to the bottom (illustration 1).

**3** Glimpse the card on the face of the pack (illustration 2). This will be the card before the selected one in the "Si Stebbins" order. Using this information you can announce the name of the selected card before the person who picked it has had a chance to look at it!

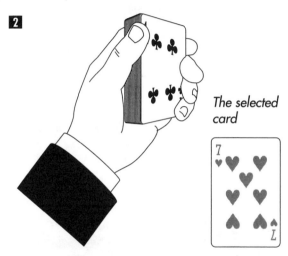

The selected card

### HISTORY OF PLAYING CARDS

*The modern-day pack of cards with its four suits and 12 court cards is based on the "Rouen" pack. This pack originated in the region of Rouen, northern France. The modern Tarot pack is now the nearest to the original Rouen pack.*

## ♠ TRIPLE REVELATION ♣

**Effect** *A pack of cards is freely cut and three cards removed. The magician correctly reveals the names of the three cards.*

**Requirements** *You need a full pack of 52 cards.*

**Preparation** *Set up the cards in the "Si Stebbins" order.*

●●●●●●●●●●●●●●●●

**1**

*The spectator cuts the pack.*

A                    B

### TOP TIPS FOR TRICKSTERS

*Don't call your props "normal" or "ordinary" – it only arouses suspicion.*

**2**

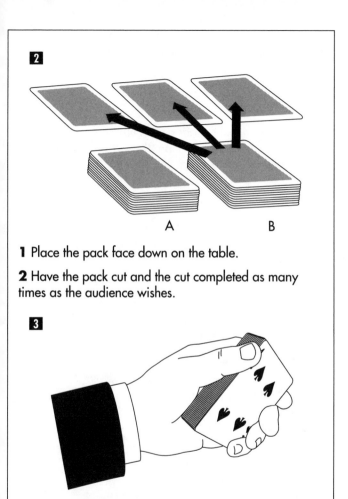

A          B

**1** Place the pack face down on the table.

**2** Have the pack cut and the cut completed as many times as the audience wishes.

**3**

**3** Now ask a spectator to cut the pack wherever they wish (illustration 1).

**4** Deal the first three cards from pile B face down on to the table (illustration 2).

**5** Pick up the rest of the pack and glimpse the card at the bottom of pile A (illustration 3) which was above the three selected cards – which you now name!

*The three selected cards.*

### JUAN TAMARIZ

*Tamariz is a graduate of the Spanish magical community and is considered to be one of the most talented and entertaining card magicians alive today. Although it is for his high level of technique with a pack of cards that he is known and respected by magicians around the world, in his home country the Spanish public know and love him for his crazy, frenetic style and the enthusiasm he displays on his television specials.*

**Effect** *The magician deals four hands from a pack of cards. The magician manages to beat three strong hands with a royal flush!*

**Requirements** *You need a full pack of 52 cards.*

**Preparation** *Set up the pack in "Si Stebbins" order.*

● ● ● ● ● ● ● ● ● ● ● ● ● ● ● ●

**1** Ask for the pack to be cut – and the cut completed – several times.

**2** Take back the cards and cut any Two-value card to the face of the pack. The suit of this card will be the suit of your winning hand (illustration 1).

**3** Have four hands of five cards each dealt out. Make sure the fourth hand is dealt to you.

**4** The first hand will have a strong flush, as will the second and third (illustrations 2, 3 and 4). These are all

### TOP TIPS FOR TRICKSTERS

*It is a good idea to check that your props work okay just prior to a performance, even if they were fine the last time you used them.*

good betting hands. Ask if anyone would like to make a bet. After all, so far everything has been carried out as it would be in a real Las Vegas casino – the cards have been freely cut several times and have been correctly dealt out by an impartial dealer (watch out for any

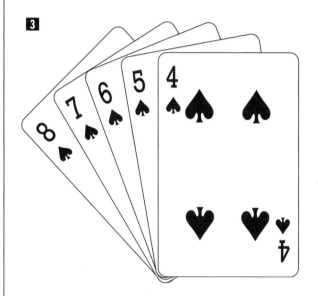

**3**

---

**TOP TIPS FOR TRICKSTERS**

*Don't worry if a trick goes wrong – Tommy Cooper, the famous British magician, was loved by audiences BECAUSE his tricks went wrong!*

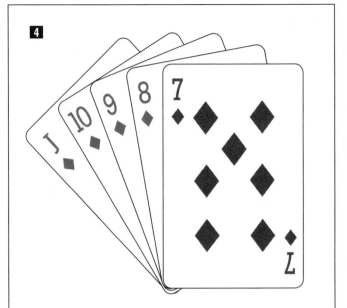

**4**

bottom or second dealing!). You may find that somebody is willing to gamble – even better!

**5** After all the other hands have been revealed slowly turn your cards over, one at a time, to reveal that you

### TOP TIPS FOR TRICKSTERS

*If you want to put a few tricks together to make an act, remember that the opening trick should ideally be short and exciting, not involving the use of volunteers.*

have the highest possible hand – the Ten, Jack, Queen, King and Ace all of the same suit – a royal flush! Grab your winnings and head for the door!

**5**

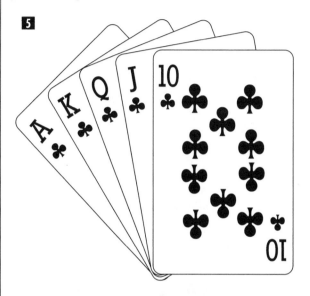

### WALTER B. GIBSON

*An American writer with a love of card magic, Gibson ghost-wrote magic books for Houdini (who was a close friend), Thurston and Blackstone. He also wrote books for which he was credited. His* Complete Illustrated Book of Close-up Magic *is highly recommended.*

# CARD CLASSICS

**Effect** *A chosen card is torn into quarters and burnt – apart from one corner which is kept back. The card is found restored in the magician's pocket – and the torn corner fits exactly!*

**Requirements** *You need a full pack of 52 cards and some matches.*

**Preparation** *Tear a corner off one card – we will assume it is the Joker. Discard the torn corner and set the Joker on the face of the pack as in illustration 1, with the torn section in the bottom lefthand corner.*

**1**

**1** Spread or fan the cards face down for one to be selected.

**2** Keep the squared up pack face down in your left hand (the dealer's grip). Your left fingers will conceal the torn corner of the Joker. Take the selected card (we will assume it is the Five of Diamonds) and tear off the upper righthand corner. Try to match the tear with that on the Joker. Hand the torn corner of the Five of Diamonds to a spectator for safe keeping.

**3** Turn the pack face towards you (be careful that nobody sees that the face card has a torn corner). Hold the pack so that the Joker's torn section is in the bottom left corner. Place the Five of Diamonds on the face of the pack with the torn section in the top right corner. This will cover the tear in the Joker (illustration 2).

**4** You say that you have put the card on the pack so that a spectator can sign their name across the face of

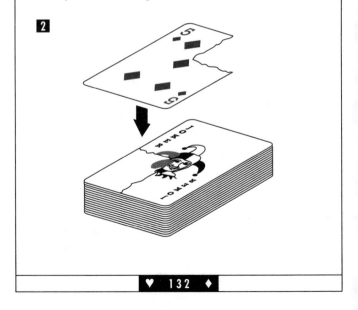

**2**

**3**

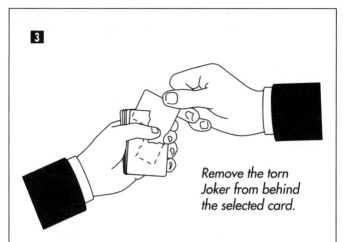

*Remove the torn Joker from behind the selected card.*

the card. When they have done this, you turn the pack face towards you and apparently remove the selected card. In reality you take the duplicate torn card (the Joker). As you can see from illustration 3 this is easy because you just pull it through the gap provided by the torn corner. Keep this card back towards the audience – they must not know this is not the selection. They will assume that it is the selected card because of the torn corner. Place the rest of the pack in an empty pocket.

**5** Keeping the card with its back towards the audience, tear it up into little pieces and burn them. When the pieces have all burnt reach into your pocket and pull out the selected card. The corner the spectator has been holding on to fits exactly.

# ♠ RISING CARD ♣

**Effect** *A selected card rises from the pack inside the card case.*

**Requirements** *You will need a full pack of 52 cards and the card case or box.*

**Preparation** *There is no preparation for this effect.*

● ● ● ● ● ● ● ● ● ● ● ● ● ● ● ●

**1**

*Chosen card*

**1** Have a card freely selected from the face-down pack.

**2** Glimpse the bottom card. Use this as a key card to find the selected card after it has been cut to the center of the pack.

**3** Under cover of the back of the left hand, push down the cards either side of the selection (illustration 1).

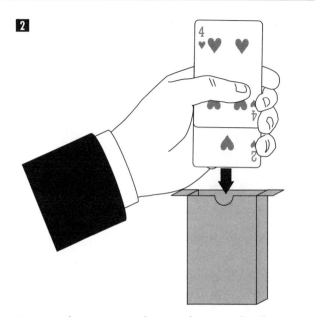

**4** Keeping the two protruding cards covered with your left hand, slide the pack into the card case (illustration 2), leaving it sticking out about half way. You then hold the pack in this position by squeezing it through the box

### TOP TIPS FOR TRICKSTERS

*Try to pace your act – intersperse short tricks with longer routines (such as effects involving a lot of dealing). This will lend more variety to your show.*

(illustration 3). Ask the spectator who selected the card to hold on to the card case in exactly the same way as you are doing – squeezing the pack to hold it in position sticking out of the box. Tell them that you will count to three and then they must shout out loud the name of the card that they selected. At the same time they must release their pressure on the card case so that the cards fall down into the box.

### TOP TIPS FOR TRICKSTERS

*Unless you are an expert it is probably not a good idea to do a performance made up entirely of card tricks. Try to use a variety of items as props.*

**5** When they release the pressure all the cards will drop down into the case – except for one card which will appear to rise out (illustration 4). This will be the chosen

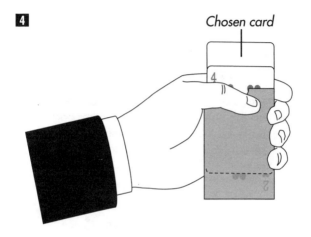

*Chosen card*

card! It will appear that the magic has happened in the spectator's own hands. This is a really surprising effect. Try it on yourself and you will see how amazing it is!

### TOP TIPS FOR TRICKSTERS

*Quieter moments in your performance are necessary to provide contrast. This is a good time to ask for volunteers to help you with your tricks.*

**Effect** *A spectator and the magician each select a card from a pack. Amazingly their two selections match!*

**Requirements** *For this you will need two full packs of 52 cards.*

**Preparation** *There is no preparation for this effect.*

● ● ● ● ● ● ● ● ● ● ● ● ● ● ● ●

**1** Ask a spectator to choose either pack and shuffle it (we will call this pack A). You take the other pack and shuffle it (pack B). When you have finished shuffling glimpse the card on the bottom of pack B (illustration 1).

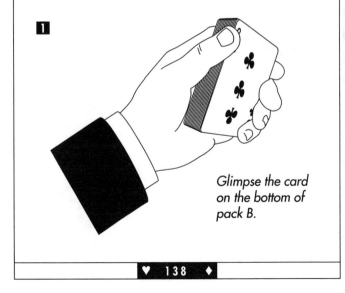

*Glimpse the card on the bottom of pack B.*

**2** Now swap packs.

**3** Ask the spectator to fan through their pack (pack B) and remove any card they wish. You do the same with pack A. Neither of you allows anyone to look at your cards.

**4** Ask the spectator to replace their card on top of their pack (pack B) and cut it to the middle. This places their card next to your key card! You do the same with your selected card.

**2**

*Spectator's chosen card*

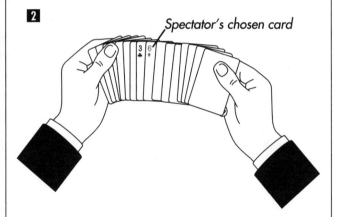

**5** Swap the packs back again. Ask the spectator to go through pack A and remove the card they chose and place it face down on the table. You say that you will do the same with your pack (pack B).

**6** What you really do is to go through pack B and take out the card above your key card. This will be the spectator's selection (illustration 2). Place it face down on the table.

**7** Turn both cards face up. Incredibly they match (illustration 3) – it seems that you both chose the same card!

 *The chosen cards are identical.*

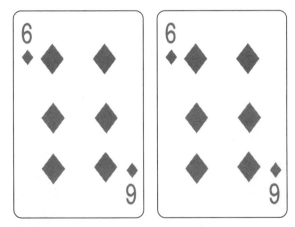

---

### TOP TIPS FOR TRICKSTERS

*Save your most spectacular effect for last. Try not to use volunteers from the audience for this trick, so that you can take your bow and make a quick exit!*

**Effect** *A selected card penetrates through the centre of a handkerchief.*

**Requirements** *You need a full pack of 52 cards, plus a thick card and a large opaque handkerchief or headsquare.*

**Preparation** *Begin with the thick card face down on top of the pack.*

● ● ● ● ● ● ● ● ● ● ● ● ● ● ● ●

**1** Have a card selected and replaced face down on top of the pack, on top of the thick card.

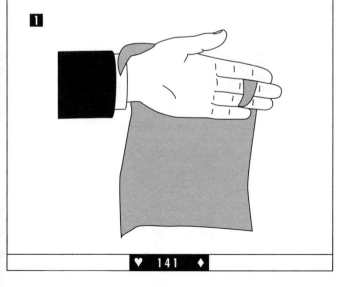

**2** Have the cards cut, and complete the cut to lose the selected card in the middle of the pack. The magician now cuts at the thick card. This moves the selected card to the bottom of the pack. Drape the handkerchief over your left wrist (illustration 1), clipping the corner between your fingers so that your thumb is free.

**3** Hold the pack in your right hand by one end, keeping the face of the pack towards you. Now you are going to drape the handkerchief over the pack, while secretly taking the selected card in the left hand.

**5** As the pack passes behind your left hand, your left thumb peels the selected card from the bottom of the

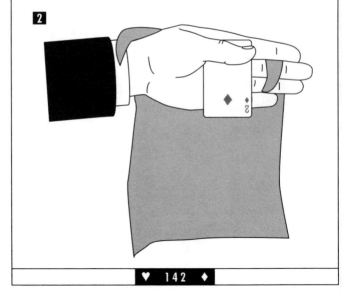

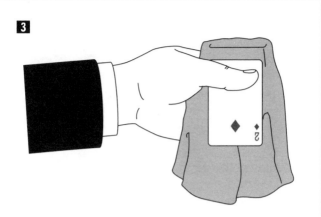

pack and grips it. All this is concealed from your audience by the handkerchief (illustration 2).

**7** Continue moving the pack into the handkerchief and lift it up inside the handkerchief so that it is completely draped. Release the clipped corner of the handkerchief. The card still in your left hand is concealed by the wrapped pack. Move the wrapped pack back towards your left hand and add the concealed card to the outside of the handkerchief (illustration 3).

---

**TOP TIPS FOR TRICKSTERS**

*The most important rule in producing an act is to remember that audiences will never complain if an act is too short – always leave them wanting more!*

---

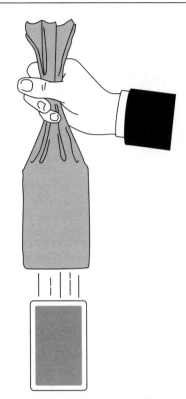

**8** Hold the pack through the folds of the handkerchief with the left hand and grab the corners of the handkerchief with the right hand. Shake the handkerchief with the right hand, letting go with the left. The selected card will fall out, apparently penetrating the material (illustration 4).

# BASIC CARD CONTROLS

*This section describes two different ways that you can "control" a selected card so that you know its position in the pack. The first control is known as "The Crimp."*

•••••••••••••••••

**1** "The Crimp" is the name for a secret bend in a playing card. The easiest way to secretly put a small bend in a playing card is to hold the pack in your left hand and pull down on the bottom righthand corner of the bottom card with your left little finger to bend it slightly (illustration 1).

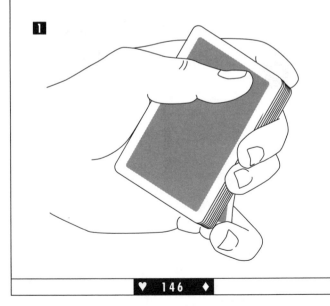

**2** Even if the cards are given a cut you can still find the crimped card in the pack (illustration 2). Make sure that when the crimped card is in the pack you keep the crimped end away from the audience.

**3** The gap in the pack created by the Crimp is known as a "Break." You will find it easy to cut to the break, and then cut the crimped card back to the bottom.

**4** To use this control in an effect, ask for a card to be freely selected from the pack. While the audience are noting the card, square up the pack in the left hand and crimp the bottom card of the pack. Have the selected card placed face down on top of the pack. Ask a member of your audience to cut the cards and complete the cut, apparently losing the selected card in the middle of the pack. The selected card is now below the crimped card. So, by cutting to the break you can secretly cut the selection back to the top of the pack.

Alternatively, by crimping the top card of the pack you can control the selection to the bottom of the pack.

*The most popular, and probably the easiest, way to shuffle cards is the "Overhand Shuffle." In this you cut a pile of cards from the back half of the pack with the right hand and peel them off on to the top of the rest of the pack with the left thumb (illustration 1).*

*This control is a false version of that shuffle. It will enable you to find a selected card apparently lost randomly in the shuffle.*

● ● ● ● ● ● ● ● ● ● ● ● ● ● ● ●

**1**

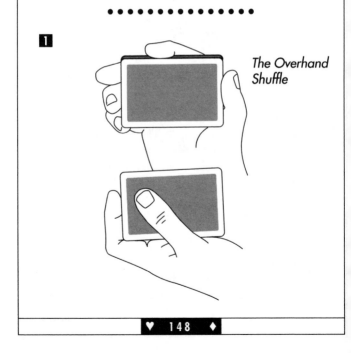

*The Overhand Shuffle*

**1** Have a card selected and while its value is being noted give the rest of the pack a genuine overhand shuffle.

**2** Now cut off some cards from the bottom of the pack with the right hand and hold out the left hand for the selected card to be replaced on top.

**3** Now you are going to "injog" the next card. The left thumb peels off the top card of the righthand pile but does not pull it square on to the lefthand pile. This card

**3**

is left "injogged" towards you, sticking out over the back end of the pile by about 1cm/0.5in (illustration 3).

**4** Now shuffle the rest of the cards in the right hand on top. As you do this ensure that you do not knock the injogged card square with the pack.

### TOP TIPS FOR TRICKSTERS

*It is a good idea to write down a list of the tricks you have performed and make a note of any comments you have to improve them at a later date.*

**5** When the shuffle has been completed and all the cards from the right hand are shuffled on top you can display the cards on your left hand. Concealed at the end of the pack pointing towards you is one card slightly sticking out. This is your injogged card and the one below it is the selected card.

**6** Your right hand comes over the pack to give it a cut. It is easy to cut at the selected card by bringing the thumb to the back end of the pack and pulling up on the injogged card (illustration 4).

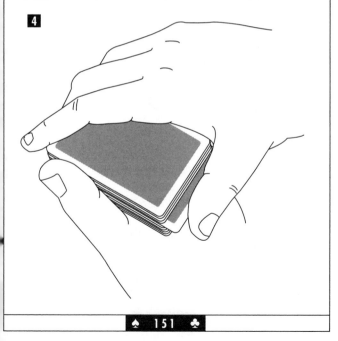

**7** Cut this half of the pack to the bottom. The selected card will now be on top of the pack.

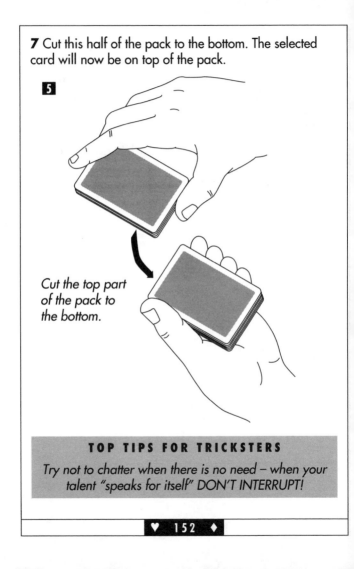

**5**

*Cut the top part of the pack to the bottom.*

### TOP TIPS FOR TRICKSTERS

*Try not to chatter when there is no need – when your talent "speaks for itself" DON'T INTERRUPT!*

**Effect** *A selected card, that is apparently lost in the center of the pack, adheres to the magician's finger and rises mysteriously out of the pack.*

**Requirements** *A full pack of 52 cards.*

**Preparation** *None.*

• • • • • • • • • • • • • • • •

**1** Have a card selected, replaced and control it to the top of the pack (use one of the Basic Card Controls already described).

**1**

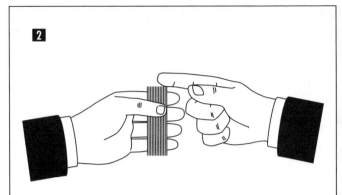

**2** Hold the cards in the left hand (illustration 1), with the faces towards your audience.

**3** Point your right first finger towards the audience and rub it backwards and forwards across the top short edge of the pack (illustration 2). Explain that you are magnetising the cards.

**4** Hidden behind the pack your right hand secretly extends its little finger (illustration 3).

**5** Hold the right hand still and allow the little finger to contact the back of the top card (the selection).

---

**TOP TIPS FOR TRICKSTERS**

*There is no reward for having talent, only for using it.*

---

**6** Slowly lift your right hand straight up about 5cm/2in. Because of your little finger the chosen card will rise up. It will appear to be mysteriously adhering to your right first finger – it seems that the magical magnetic attraction has worked!

**3**

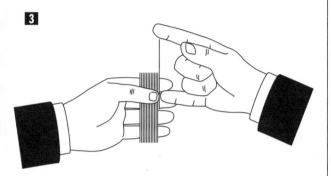

### KEN BROOKE (1920-1983)

*Ken Brooke was an Englishman man famed among magicians for his ability to sell them anything. He was what is known as a magical demonstrator, performing the latest tricks which were for sale. At magic conventions and gatherings his stand always had the largest crowds because of his quick wit and charm. He was known especially for his performance of "Chase the Ace" – a version of the Three Card Trick with large playing cards created for use on a big stage.*

**Effect** *A card is freely selected. The card is shuffled into the pack which is replaced in the card case. The card case is dropped into an empty envelope, and the envelope is pierced with a pencil. Despite the impossible situation, the selected card appears spiked on the pencil!*

**Requirements** *A pack of cards and card case, a long envelope which opens on one of the short edges and a sharp pencil.*

**Preparation** *None.*

• • • • • • • • • • • • • • •

**1** Have a card freely selected from the pack. Control the card to the top of the pack using one of the Basic Card

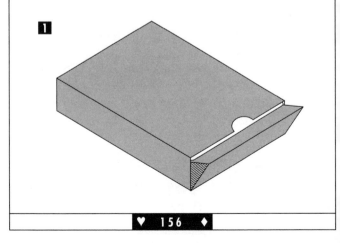

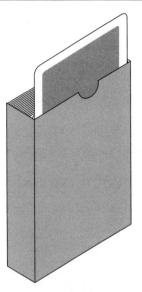

Controls. Place the pack in the card case with the top card (the selection) next to the half moon cut out in the case.

**2** Squeeze the case at the sides so that the first few cards at the top of the pack bow outwards. You are going to close the flap on the case, but insert it between the top two cards (illustration 1). The bow in the cards makes this easier. A portion of the back of the selected card can now be seen in the half moon cut out in the case. Keep your right thumb on this.

**3** Show the envelope is empty and drop the case inside. As you do this, keep gripping the selected card with your right thumb. The selected card should slip out of the case (illustration 2) and be held inside the top of the envelope between the right thumb and the left hand outside the envelope. When the left hand is holding it securely remove your right hand.

**4** Push the sharp pencil through the top of the envelope. This spikes the selected card (illustration 3). Ask a spectator to hold the pencil tightly and pull down on the case inside the envelope. The envelope will rip, revealing the impaled selected card.

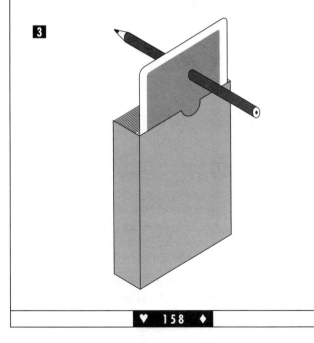

A
Ace Sandwich, 113-116
Advanced tricks
    basic card controls, 145-158
    can't go wrong, 82-93
    card classics, 130-144
    controlling cards, 101-116
    forces, 94-100
    the stacked pack, 117-129

B
Big effects, 72-78
    Cards Across, 73-75
    Comical Card Trick, 76-78
Brooke, Ken, 155

C
Calculator Card, 42-44
Cardini, 20
Card On Window, 99-100
Cards Across, 73-75
Cards In Pocket, 110-112
Card Stab, 156-158
Classic tricks
Card Through Handkerchief, 141-144
    Do As I Do, 138-140
    Rising Card, 134-137
    Torn and Restored Card, 131-133
Clock Tower Card, 27-29
Comical Card Trick, 76-78
Controls
    Ace Sandwich, 113-116
    basic, 145-158
Cards In Pocket, 110-112
Card Stab, 156-158
The Crimp, 146-147
    Lie Detector, 102-105

Magnetised Cards, 153-155
    The Next Card I Turn Over, 106-109
    Overhand Shuffle, 148-152
The Crimp, 146-147
Cutting The Aces, 83-86

D
Do As I Do, 138-140
Duck and Deal, 16-20

E
Elmsley, Alex, 105
Erdnase, S.W., 58

F
Fake cards, 30--53
Calculator Card, 42-44
Find The Lady, 38-41
    Joker's Wild, 34-37
    Kings To Aces, 45-48
    Queens To Fours, 31-33
    Scarlet Pimpernel, 49-53
Faulty Follower, 62-65
Find The Lady, 38-41
Forces
    Card On Window, 99-100
    A Little Bit Further, 95-98

G
Gemini Twins, 91-95
Gibson, Walter B., 129
The Glide, 54-71
    Faulty Follower, 62-65
    The Glide Move, 55-58
    Inseparable Aces, 69-71
    Observation Test, 66-67
    The Stop Trick, 59-61
Glossary of terms, 4-5

**H**
History, of playing cards, 95, 121
Hofzinser, Johann N., 41
Hooker Rising Cards, 9
Houdini, Harry, 12
Hugard, Jean, 48

**I**
Inseparable Aces, 69-71
The Invisible Dice, 13-15

**J**
Jay, Ricky, 61
Joker's Wild, 34-37

**K**
"King of Kards," 12
Kings To Aces, 45-48

**L**
Las Vegas Poker Deal, 125-129
Leipsig, Nate, 86
Lie Detector, 102-105
A Little Bit Further, 95-98

**M**
Magnetised Cards, 153-155

**N**
The Next Card I Turn Over, 106-109

**O**
Observation Test, 66-67
Odd One Out, 10-12
One Way Cards, 21-23
Overhand Shuffle Control, 148-152

**Q**
Queens To Fours, 31-33

**R**
Rising Card, 134-137
"Rouen" pack, 121

**S**
Scarlet Pimpernel, 49-53
Self-working tricks, 6-29
    Clock Tower Card, 27-29
    Duck and Deal, 16-20
    The Invisible Dice, 13-15
    Odd One Out, 10-12
    One Way Cards, 21-23
The Seven Card Poker Hand, 7-9
The Seven Pile Trick, 24-26
The Seven Card Poker Hand, 7-9
The Seven Pile Trick, 24-26
The Stack, 118-119
Stacked Selection, 120-121
The Stop Trick, 59-61

**T**
Tamariz, Juan, 124
Tips for tricksters. See under specific tricks
Torn and Restored Card, 131-133
Triple Revelation, 122-124

**V**
Vernon, Dai, 37

**Y**
You Are The Magician, 87-90